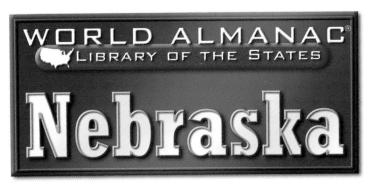

Nebraska

THE CORNHUSKER STATE

by Michael E. Flocker

Curriculum Consultant: Jean Craven,
Director of Instructional Support,
Albuquerque, NM, Public Schools

WORLD ALMANAC® LIBRARY

Please visit our web site at: **www.worldalmanaclibrary.com**
For a free color catalog describing World Almanac® Library's
list of high-quality books and multimedia programs, call
1-800-848-2928 (USA) or 1-800-387-3178 (Canada).
World Almanac® Library's fax: (414) 332-3567.

Library of Congress Cataloging-in-Publication Data

Flocker, Michael.
        Nebraska, the Cornhusker State/ by Michael Flocker.
            p. cm. — (World Almanac Library of the states)
        Includes bibliographical references and index.
        Summary: Surveys the history, land, economy, politics and government,
    culture, and notable people and events of Nebraska.
        ISBN 0-8368-5140-4 (lib. bdg.)
        ISBN 0-8368-5310-5 (softcover)
        1. Nebraska—Juvenile literature. [1. Nebraska.] I. Title. II. Series.
    F666.3.F57   2002
    978.2—dc21   2002023490

This edition first published in 2002 by
World Almanac® Library
330 West Olive Street, Suite 100
Milwaukee, WI 53212 USA

This edition © 2002 by World Almanac® Library.

Design and Editorial: Bill SMITH STUDIO Inc.
Editor: Timothy Paulson
Assistant Editor: Megan Elias
Art Director: Jay Jaffe
Photo Research: Sean Livingstone

World Almanac® Library Project Editor: Patricia Lantier
World Almanac® Library Editors: Catherine Gardner, Lyman Lyons, Monica Rausch,
 Jim Mezzanotte
World Almanac® Library Production: Scott M. Krall, Tammy Gruenewald,
 Katherine A. Goedheer

Photo credits: pp. 4-5 © PhotoDisc; p. 6 (all) © Corel; p. 7 (all) © University of Nebraska; p. 9
© ArtToday; p. 10 © CORBIS; p. 11 © Corel; p. 12 © Library of Congress; p. 13 © Library of
Congress; p. 14 © Dover; p. 15 © Library of Congress; p. 17 © Library of Congress; p. 18
© PhotoDisc; p. 19 © Greater Omaha CVB; p. 20 (left to right) © PAINET INC., © Corel; p. 21
(left to right) © PAINET INC., © ArtToday, © Corel, © Library of Congress; p. 23 © Corel; p. 25
© PhotoDisc; p. 27 © Hunter Public Relations; p. 29 © Phillip Gould/CORBIS; p. 30 © Dover;
p. 31 (all) © Library of Congress; p. 32 © PAINET INC.; p. 33 © Corel; p. 34 (all) © Greater Omaha
CVB; p. 35 © Greater Omaha CVB; p. 36 © Greater Omaha CVB; p. 39 (bottom) © PhotoDisc,
(top) © Dover; p. 40 © PhotoDisc; p. 41 © PhotoDisc; pp. 42-43 © Library of Congress; p. 44
(bottom left) © PhotoDisc, (top right) © Corel; p. 45 (center) © Greater Omaha CVB, (bottom
right) © PhotoDisc

Printed in the United States of America

1 2 3 4 5 6 7 8 9 06 05 04 03 02

Nebraska

Land of the Pioneers

Nebraska is a land of wide-open spaces, and the spirit of its people is as expansive as the plains. Before European settlement, Native Americans lived off the herds of bison that roamed the vast prairies. The first Europeans to settle the region came in small numbers, but the Kansas-Nebraska Act of 1854 and the Homestead Act of 1862 threw the region open to settlement. Thousands of hopeful pioneers came to sink their roots in Nebraska soil. Those who made their homes in Nebraska had dreams as big as the prairie sky, but they were willing to start off in houses made of sod. Nebraskan Willa Cather celebrated that pioneer spirit in her novels. Whole families worked together to establish claims, and claims grew into farms. Farms grew into an agricultural industry that today supplies food to millions of people around the world.

In the late nineteenth century, that same spirit of industry and self-reliance helped shape U.S. politics. During the populist movement, Nebraska farmers banded together to protect their interests. William Jennings Bryan, a Nebraska representative to the U.S. Congress, stood up for the independent farmer.

Nebraskans have never been afraid to go first. Susan LaFlesche Picotte became the first Native American woman to earn a medical degree, and Julius Sterling Morton began the tradition of Arbor Day. Nebraska is the first and only state to buck the tradition of the two-party political system and the two-house legislature. The state's unicameral legislature and no-party ballot throw the field wide open for individual opinions and innovation.

Proving that anything is possible in the wide-open spaces of Nebraska, the state is home to the world's largest indoor desert and the largest indoor rain forest, as well as the record-breaking Cornhuskers football team. The Nebraskan "the sky's the limit" spirit challenges its people to dare as much as they dream.

▶ Map of Nebraska showing the interstate highway system, as well as major cities and waterways.

▼ Scotts Bluff, in Nebraska, overlooks remnants of the Oregon Trail.

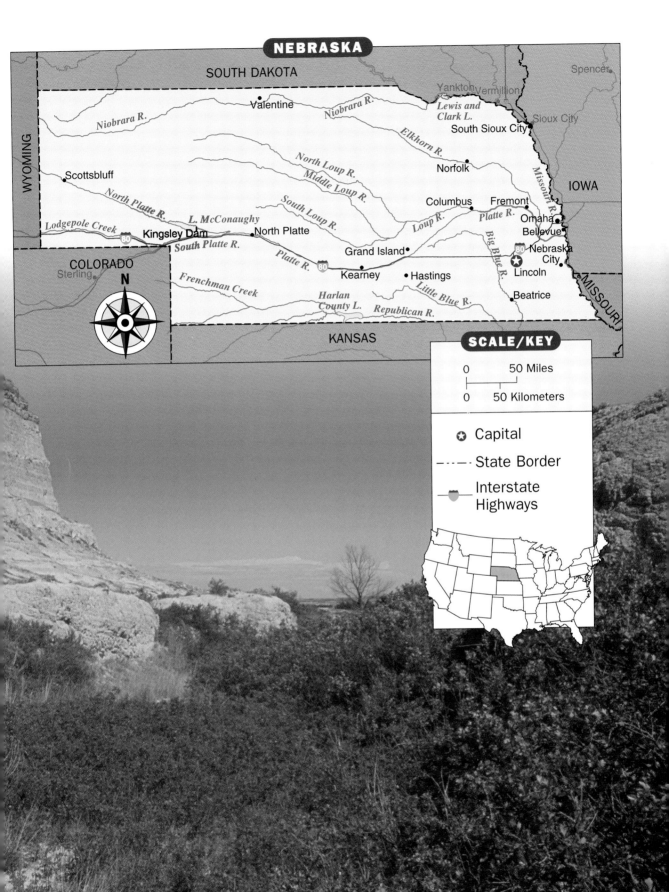

SOUTH DAKOTA

Spencer

Valentine

Niobrara R.

Niobrara R.

Yankton Vermillion

Lewis and
Clark L.

Sioux City

South Sioux City

WYOMING

Scottsbluff

North Loup R.

Middle Loup R.

Elkhorn R.

Norfolk

IOWA

North Platte R.

South Loup R.

Columbus

Fremont

Lodgepole Creek

L. McConaughy

Kingsley Dam

North Platte

South Platte R.

Loup R.

Platte R.

Omaha
Bellevue

Missouri R.

Big Blue R.

Nebraska
City

Lincoln

COLORADO

Sterling

South Platte R.

Platte R.

Grand Island

Kearney

Hastings

MISSOURI

N

Frenchman Creek

Harlan
County L.

Little Blue R.

Beatrice

Republican R.

KANSAS

Fast Facts
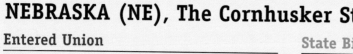

NEBRASKA (NE), The Cornhusker State

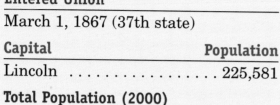

Entered Union

March 1, 1867 (37th state)

Capital   **Population**

Lincoln 225,581

Total Population (2000)

1,711,263 (38th most populous state)
— *Between 1990 and 2000, the
population of Nebraska increased
8.4 percent.*

Largest Cities	Population
Omaha	390,007
Lincoln	225,581
Bellevue	44,382
Grand Island	42,940
Kearney	27,431

Land Area

76,872 square miles (199,098 square
kilometers) (15th largest state)

State Motto

"Equality Before the Law"

State Song

"Beautiful Nebraska," *by Jim Fras
and Guy G. Miller, adopted in 1967.*

State Mammal

White-tailed deer — *Although
Nebraska was once known as
the Antelope State, it adopted
the white-tailed deer as its
official mammal in 1981.*

State Bird

Western meadowlark — *This yellow-
breasted bird with black and white
spots was chosen by the state's
children in 1928.*

State Fish

Channel catfish — *Found in lakes
and rivers and bred in fish farms,
the channel catfish is a popular
sport fish.*

State Insect

Honeybee — *The honeybee was
chosen as the state insect in 1975
because of its importance in
agriculture and because Nebraska
is a major producer of honey.*

State Flower

Goldenrod

State Tree

Cottonwood —
*Cottonwoods grow
throughout the
state and, in the
days of the pioneers, were
often used as landmarks.*

State Gem

Blue chalcedony — *This pale stone
with bands of blue and white is an
agate, and it is frequently used in
making jewelry.*

State Soft Drink

Kool-Aid — *This powdered drink
mix was invented in Hastings in 1927.*

PLACES TO VISIT

Carhenge, *Alliance*
In 1987, a large extended family got together in Alliance to build a re-creation of one of Europe's most famous monuments — Stonehenge. Stonehenge is an ancient, giant circle of massive, square-topped stone arches. Instead of stones, the Nebraska families used cars of all makes and models and painted them gray for a stony effect.

Crane Meadows Nature Center, *Grand Island*
Every spring bird-watchers travel to Grand Island to see the largest gathering of sandhill cranes in the world. More than five hundred thousand cranes come to the area on their way north after spending the winter in the south. Visitors also can enjoy wildflowers blooming on the prairie.

Strategic Air and Space Museum, *Ashland*
Visitors can see a large collection of historical airplanes and missiles, as well as an interactive gallery and exhibits on subjects such as space travel and the Central Intelligence Agency.

For other places and events, see p. 44.

BIGGEST, BEST, AND MOST

- The world's largest porch swing hangs in the Hebron city park.

- The biggest train robbery in the history of the Union Pacific Railroad took place in Big Springs, where Express Train No. 4 was robbed in 1877.

- Cozad ships more alfalfa than any other place in the United States. Alfalfa is a plant that is used to feed livestock.

STATE FIRSTS

- **1882** Buffalo Bill Cody held the first rodeo in U.S. history in North Platte.

- **1972** Part of 15th Street in Omaha became the first road in the nation to be paved with glasphalt, a combination of crushed glass and paving asphalt.

Native American Pioneer

Susan LaFlesche Picotte, daughter of Iron Eye, chief of the Omaha Indians, became the first Native American woman to earn a medical degree. Picotte grew up on the Omaha reservation in northeastern Nebraska. She attended schools in New Jersey and Virginia before graduating from the Women's Medical College of Pennsylvania in 1889. Picotte was first in her class. After graduation, she returned to Nebraska to provide medical care to Omaha children and adults and was an active member of her community until she died in 1915 in Walthill.

Tractor Pull

The University of Nebraska at Lincoln is home to the most prestigious tractor-testing laboratory in the United States. It is the officially designated tractor-testing station for the country. The laboratory opened in 1920 and ensures that tractors conform to a set of international standards. In addition to the lab, there is also a tractor museum. Lester F. Larsen, who was the chief engineer of the station from 1946 to 1975, collected the museum's historic tractors.

Gateway to the West

> What I am sure of is there is not any gold nor any other metal in all that country, and the other things of which they had told me are nothing but little villages, and in many of these they do not plant anything and do not have any houses except of skins and sticks, and they wander around with the cows.
>
> — Francisco Vásquez de Coronado,
> Spanish explorer on the Great Plains, 1510–1554

The wide-open land now known as Nebraska was home to many nomadic peoples over the course of ten thousand years. Antelope, elk, and bison (also known as buffalo) roamed the rolling hills and vast prairies. Archaeologists think that for a period of about two hundred years, until about A.D. 600, Nebraska was populated by people who hunted these animals and practiced simple forms of agriculture. Eventually, for reasons that are unknown, they were replaced by a culture that relied more heavily on agriculture.

During the last five hundred years, various Native American groups have lived in the Nebraska region. The Omaha and Oto settled in the eastern part of the state, while the Pawnee and Ponca lived in the central plains area. The Pawnee farmed beans, corn, and squash. Twice a year, they would leave their villages to hunt large game, including bison. Toward the west, the region that leads into present-day Colorado and Wyoming was home to the Dakota, also known as the Sioux. The Arapaho and Cheyenne lived in this region, too. These western groups were nomadic hunters who had frequent disputes with the Pawnee over territory.

Spain and France

In 1540, the Spanish explorer Francisco Vásquez de Coronado led an expedition of about three hundred Spaniards, hundreds of Indians, and Native slaves north from Compostela, Mexico. In 1541, they reached the plains of central North America. Coronado had heard of mythical

Native Americans of Nebraska
Arapaho
Cheyenne
Dakota (Sioux)
Omaha
Oto
Pawnee
Ponca
Santee (Sioux)
Winnebago

DID YOU KNOW?

The state's name comes from the Oto name for the Platte River, *Nebrathka*, which means "flat water." Not coincidentally, *plat* means "flat" in French. Both Native Americans and French explorers noticed the same quality in this river.

René-Robert Cavelier, Sieur de La Salle, was the first of a string of French explorers to visit the region that later became Nebraska. In 1682, he claimed this area as part of France's vast Louisiana Territory. Although this intrepid Frenchman mapped new lands and increased his country's holdings in North America, he was doomed never to find the original object of his search — a river passage to China.

lands rich with gold — the Seven Cities of Cibola and the Kingdom of Quivira — and sought them unsuccessfully. Whether Coronado reached Nebraska is debatable, but his quest for gold is part of state legend.

French explorer René-Robert Cavelier, Sieur de La Salle, journeyed down the Mississippi River in 1682 and claimed all the land drained by that river in the name of France. He named it the province of Louisiana in honor of King Louis XIV. For many years thereafter, the region attracted rugged trappers who traded with local Native Americans. In 1714, French explorer Etienne Veniard de Bourgmont traveled up the Missouri River to the mouth of what later became known as the Platte River. There, he built a trading post. Bourgmont was the first European known to have actually set foot in Nebraska.

As the French continued to move westward, the Spanish objected to their presence. In 1720, a Spanish expedition was launched from Santa Fe under the leadership of Pedro de Villasur. As the soldiers traveled along the Platte River, a violent encounter with the Pawnee resulted in the massacre of de Villasur's troops. France took advantage of Spain's weakened position and used this opportunity to strengthen its claim to the region.

In 1739, two brothers from France, Pierre and Paul Mallet, crossed Nebraska. Along the way, they gave the Platte River its name. The Mallet brothers' journal is the first written description of the region.

The Louisiana Purchase

The French controlled the area that is now Nebraska until 1763, when France was defeated by Great Britain in the French and Indian War (1754–1763). Under the terms of the peace treaty, France lost its territory east of the Mississippi River to Great Britain. In a separate treaty, France gave its territory west of the Mississippi River to Spain.

Spain maintained control of this region until 1800, when the new emperor of France, Napoleon Bonaparte, demanded the territory back. Three years later, however, Napoleon sold the entire area to the United States. The transaction increased the size of the U.S. territories by more than 800,000 square miles (2,072,000 sq km). Nebraska was part of this huge land parcel that is known as the Louisiana Purchase.

Go West

President Thomas Jefferson commissioned a scientific expedition to explore the lands acquired in the Louisiana Purchase. In May 1804, explorers Meriwether Lewis and William Clark set out with a group of about thirty men.

▼ The first permanent non-Native settlement in Nebraska was Bellevue, established at the mouth of the Platte River in the 1820s.

▶ Wagons are set up in a re-enactment beside a bluff on the Oregon Trail. More than five hundred thousand pioneers passed through Nebraska on their way west.

The party trekked northward along the Missouri River in eastern Nebraska. Other explorers in Nebraska were Zebulon Pike (1806) and Stephen Long (1820). Long was unimpressed, describing the land as a "great American desert" and wrongly predicting that settlers would stay east of the Mississippi.

Traders, trappers, and explorers, followed by families, headed west in Lewis and Clark's footsteps as part of a massive migration. The first military post in Nebraska, Fort Atkinson, was established in 1819, about 16 miles (26 km) north of present-day Omaha. In the 1820s, the fur-trading post of Bellevue became the first permanent non-Native settlement in the region.

Both the California and the Oregon Trails passed through Nebraska during the mid-1800s. Many people stopped short of their final destinations and put down roots in the Nebraska region, in spite of its federal designation in 1834 as "Indian country" and a ban on non-Native settlement there.

The Kansas-Nebraska Act

Throughout the first half of the nineteenth century, the nation was bitterly divided over whether slavery should be legal in new territories. In 1820, the Missouri Compromise established a rule that all states above Missouri's southern border (except Missouri) would not allow slavery, while those below it could.

As the United States prepared to open up the Kansas and Nebraska Territories for settlement, the question of slavery became very important in the region. Stephen Douglas, a senator from Illinois, wanted the Nebraska

DID YOU KNOW?

▪ In Pawnee tradition, the Morning Star was a powerful male spirit whose helper was the Sun. The Evening Star was a powerful female spirit, and the Moon was her helper. The Morning Star and Evening Star were parents to a girl, while the Sun and Moon had a boy. Both children were swept to Earth in a whirlwind and became the first Pawnee.

Territory to be organized because he was hoping to invest in railroads in the area. If Nebraska and Kansas became official U.S. territories and eventually states, the U.S. government would help pay for the development of the railroads. Douglas was the major author of the Kansas-Nebraska Act, which the U.S. Congress passed in 1854. The act created the Nebraska and Kansas Territories and opened them to non-Native settlement. It also invalidated the Missouri Compromise by allowing state residents to decide whether a territory should allow slavery or not. The decision was to be made by a popular vote.

In Kansas, the Kansas-Nebraska Act sparked violence between pro- and antislavery settlers. Nebraska settlers, however, showed little interest in establishing slavery in their territory. The Homestead Act of 1862, passed the year after the Civil War began, gave 160 acres (65 ha) to anyone who would live on and farm the land for five years. The Homestead Act made President Abraham Lincoln very popular, encouraged large numbers of settlers to move to Nebraska, and sped the agricultural and technological development of the Midwest.

Soon the question of statehood arose. Support for joining the Union divided Nebraskans along party lines. The Republicans, who were staunchly antislavery, were in favor of joining the Union. They drew up a state constitution that they then pushed through the territorial legislature, despite opposition by Democrats. In June 1866, that document was voted on by Nebraskans and was narrowly approved.

By July 1866, Republicans in Congress were pushing to get Nebraska admitted to the Union. Vice President Andrew Johnson, a Democrat, had succeeded Lincoln to the presidency. Johnson knew that Nebraska would elect more Republicans to Congress, so he vetoed the measure.

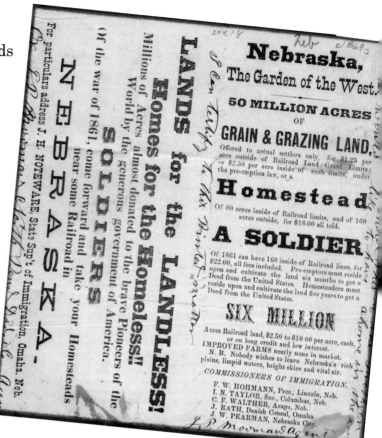

▲ An 1869 Nebraska State Department of Immigration promotion.

He was especially nervous because Republicans had tried to impeach him for not being strict enough with the defeated South. In February of the following year, Congress overrode Johnson's veto and passed a second statehood bill. The bill, however, had one condition — that Nebraska's constitution be revised to guarantee all male citizens, not just whites, the right to vote. The Nebraska legislature eventually agreed to reword the constitution.

Finally, on March 1, 1867, President Johnson reluctantly issued a proclamation that made Nebraska the thirty-seventh state. The state capital was established and named Lincoln, in honor of Abraham Lincoln, who had been assassinated two years earlier.

Railroads and Expansion

The Union Pacific Railroad began building its transcontinental line west from Omaha in 1865. By 1867, the railroad crossed the entire state. The population continued to expand, but times were difficult through the 1870s and 1880s. The state struggled; both ranches and farms suffered from droughts and grasshopper plagues.

At the end of the nineteenth century, the economy had improved. By 1890, Nebraska was home to more than one million people. A tide of European immigrants had arrived in the United States, and the face of Nebraska had begun to change.

What's in a Name?

Beginning in 1895, Nebraska was officially known as the "Tree Planters' State." The state nickname was officially changed to the "Cornhusker State" in 1945, in honor of the University of Nebraska's sports teams.

▼ This train, Burlington Engine No. 7, arrived in Broken Bow (in central Nebraska) in 1886. By the late 1880s, railroads connected many small communities across the state, bringing settlers to farms and goods to market.

The Founder of Arbor Day

Julius Sterling Morton moved to Nebraska City in 1854. Struck by the scarcity of trees there, Morton and his wife decided that the planting of trees and shrubs would make life better and their surroundings more pleasant. They put their ideas to work immediately, and the trees they planted still stand today in the Arbor Lodge State Historical Park.

Morton was the editor of the *Nebraska City News,* and he used his newspaper to spread his beliefs about the importance of planting trees. In 1872, he proposed to the State Board of Agriculture that Nebraska should observe a tree-planting holiday in April. The idea caught on, and Arbor Day was made a legal state holiday in 1885. The holiday's popularity grew, and Arbor Day is now celebrated in all fifty states and even in some foreign countries.

Morton went on to become the president of the State Board of Agriculture and eventually served as U.S. secretary of agriculture from 1893 to 1897.

Farm families continued to struggle, however. Increasing industrialization and competition from abroad hurt farmers. In response, farmers demanded tariffs on foreign goods, which would make the foreign goods more expensive. They also demanded that the federal government mint more silver money. A lawyer named William Jennings Bryan soon became the champion of the populist movement that sought to liberate the United States from relying on the gold standard by introducing silver coins.

The Native American population suffered during this period. Mass hunting of bison herds and an aggressive government policy of removing Native Americans from open country devastated the Native population. As a result, a large number of Native American people became wards of the government. This meant that U.S. governmental authorities became the legal guardians of individuals and had the right to make legal decisions on their behalf.

The Twentieth Century

In the early twentieth century, the state began to enact a number of reforms, including the regulation of child labor and the introduction of the secret ballot. Nebraska women won the right to vote in school board elections in 1883. In 1917, they were able to vote in all state elections.

The increased use of automobiles and electricity improved the quality of life throughout the United States. During World War I, Nebraska's crops brought high prices, and the state saw a brief period of prosperity.

During the 1920s, prices fell. The Great Depression, which began with the stock market crash of 1929, hit Nebraska hard. Further disaster struck in the form of an extended drought and grasshopper plagues.

As banks foreclosed on or took over farms from families who could no longer pay mortgages, farmers banded together to protect their way of life. When the banks auctioned off the foreclosed farms, neighbors gathered and refused to bid more than a few pennies, making the auctions unprofitable and often enabling farmers to regain their property. The state legislature passed a bill in 1933 to stop foreclosures, but the economy remained in bad shape until World War II.

In 1934, the state made history when it passed a constitutional amendment establishing a unicameral legislature. This meant that there was only one chamber instead of the traditional two-chamber system with a senate and a house of representatives. The amendment also specified that Nebraska state officials would be elected without any party affiliation. The first session of this new legislature was held in 1937. Just two years later, in 1939, geologists discovered oil in the southeast corner of the state, and by the early 1940s, oil had become Nebraska's most important resource.

The demand for Nebraska farm products such as potatoes, corn, and oats increased dramatically during World War II, and soon the economy was showing signs of life. More than 125,000 soldiers from Nebraska fought in the war. After World War II, the state's economic recovery continued as the federal government began to build dams to control flooding in the Midwest. Improved farming methods and advances in farming machinery lessened the demand for farm workers. Farms became larger in size but fewer in number.

During the 1980s, Nebraska's economy was struggling again, and many small farms were forced to close. In 1982, in an attempt to protect the owners of small farms, Nebraskans passed Initiative 300, a constitutional amendment that stops corporations from buying farmland or ranches in the state. An increase of jobs in the telecommunications industry had provided some economic relief by the early 1990s. Today, agriculture is still important to Nebraskans, not just economically, but as part of their heritage of old-fashioned self-reliance.

▲ This 1940 Works Progress Administration poster advocates planting trees to prevent soil erosion. When a drought struck the Midwest from 1932 to 1937, loose topsoil blew away, creating huge clouds of dust that buried farms and made agriculture nearly impossible. The area affected by the drought and dust storms came to be known as the Dust Bowl.

The Pioneer Spirit

Men came from the east and built these American towns because they wished to go no farther, and the towns they built were shaped by the urge to go onward.

— *Rose Wilder Lane, U.S. author,* Old Hometown, *1935*

In 2000, the U.S. Census revealed that Nebraska had 1,711,263 inhabitants — an average of about 22 residents per square mile (9 per sq km) of land. The population is not spread evenly throughout the state, however. The majority of residents live in the eastern region along the Missouri River or along the Platte River. The areas farther west, especially the panhandle, are much less densely populated.

Nebraska's greatest population increase happened very quickly in the years following the Civil War. In 1870, the state's population was a mere 122,993. By 1890, the population had soared to 1,058,910. This huge jump in numbers was largely due to a wave of European immigration and the availability of rail transportation from the East and West Coasts. The days of covered wagons were over, and the building of the transcontinental railroad had made it possible

Age Distribution in Nebraska
(2000 Census)

0–4	117,048
5–19	387,288
20–24	120,331
25–44	487,107
45–64	367,294
65 & over	232,195

Across One Hundred Years

Nebraska's three largest foreign-born groups for 1890 and 1990

1890 | 1990

Germany	Sweden	Bohemia
72,618	28,364	16,803

Total state population: 1,058,910
Total foreign-born: 202,542 (19%)

Mexico	Germany	United Kingdom
4,421	2,861	1,680

Total state population: 1,578,385
Total foreign-born: 28,198 (2%)

Patterns of Immigration

The total number of people who immigrated to Nebraska in 1998 was 1,267. Of that number, the largest immigrant groups were from Mexico (42.8%), India (6.9%), and Vietnam (5.6%).

for people to travel quickly across the entire country in relative comfort.

Ethnicity

By far, most of the immigrants to arrive in the late nineteenth century were from Germany, although large numbers of Swedish, English, Irish, Czech (mainly from the region called Bohemia), Danish, and Russian people also arrived on the trains from the East.

▲ A Nebraska family in Kearney posed for a photograph in 1907. The family was the key social and economic force on the Great Plains.

Although the twentieth century saw an influx of people arriving from many countries, including Mexico, Greece, and Italy, there was only slow growth in the state's population after the 1890s. In 2000, the population of Nebraska was 89.6 percent white, which is higher than the national average of 75 percent.

Religion

Many of the original communities of the pioneers were built around church groups. There were many Christian denominations represented, including Catholics, Lutherans, Mennonites, and Congregationalists. Among the early

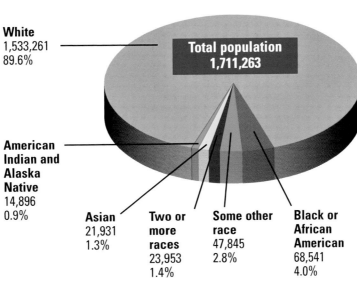

Heritage and Background, Nebraska — Year 2000

► Here's a look at the racial backgrounds of Nebraskans today. Nebraska ranks thirty-third among all U.S. states with regard to African Americans as a percentage of the population.

White
1,533,261
89.6%

**Total population
1,711,263**

American Indian and Alaska Native
14,896
0.9%

Native Hawaiian and other Pacific Islander
836
less than 0.1%

Asian
21,931
1.3%

Two or more races
23,953
1.4%

Some other race
47,845
2.8%

Black or African American
68,541
4.0%

Note: 5.5% (94,425) of the population identify themselves as **Hispanic** or **Latino,** a cultural designation that crosses racial lines. Hispanics and Latinos are counted in this category as well as the racial category of their choice.

Nebraskan Catholics were Irish, Polish, Czech, and Italian immigrants, while Lutheran settlers were mostly German, Danish, and Swedish.

Today, Catholics, Lutherans, and Methodists are the largest religious groups in Nebraska. Jewish Nebraskans make up about 0.5 percent of the population, and Hindus 0.2 percent. Buddhists and agnostics (people who neither believe nor disbelieve in God) are each 0.1 percent of the population. The number of Nebraskans who are Muslim comes to less than 0.1 percent of the population, but there are at least three Islamic centers in the state.

Educational Levels of Nebraska Workers (age 25 and over)	
Less than 9th grade	79,925
9th to 12th grade, no diploma	101,147
High school graduate, including equivalency	345,778
Some college, no degree or associate degree	280,537
Bachelor's degree	130,172
Graduate or professional degree	58,490

▼ The skyline of Omaha, Nebraska's largest city.

► Students in Gretna take a field trip to learn about Nebraska agriculture.

Education

In the 1820s, the first schools were opened for white settlers. School districts and school boards were established in the Nebraska Territory in 1855 when the legislature passed the free school law. The state constitution of 1875 included secondary schools in the educational system.

Today, Nebraska state law requires that all children attend school from the ages of seven to sixteen. Census figures indicate that among Nebraskans over the age of twenty-five, more than 80 percent have high school diplomas and roughly 20 percent hold college degrees.

There are approximately thirty-five institutions of higher education in Nebraska. The most prominent of these is the University of Nebraska, with campuses in Lincoln, Omaha, and Kearney and a medical center in Omaha. Other large colleges and universities include Peru State College in Peru, Creighton University in Omaha, Hastings College in Hastings, Wayne State College in Wayne, and Nebraska Wesleyan University in Lincoln.

Where Do Nebraskans Live?

About two-thirds of Nebraska's population lives in urban areas. Omaha and Lincoln are by far the two largest cities in the state, and both are located in the populous eastern third of the state. Omaha is the state's industrial trade center and one of the nation's chief railway centers. Lincoln is an education, government, and retail center.

The central part of the state is largely farmland. The residents of the western half of the state, where ranches are more numerous than farms, embrace the attire, recreational activities, and manners of the Western lifestyle often associated with neighboring Colorado and Wyoming. Cowboy hats and rodeos are commonplace in these parts.

Founder of Boys Town

A native of Ireland, Father Edward J. Flanagan was a Roman Catholic priest who came to Nebraska in 1912. He took a position as an assistant pastor at St. Patrick's Church in Omaha and began working with the poor and destitute. On December 12, 1917, he founded the Home for Homeless Boys. In 1921 Flanagan purchased Overlook Farm, which later was named Boys Town.

Boys Town was a self-contained community where homeless or disadvantaged boys could find a home, get an education, and learn a trade. Today, there are Boys and Girls Towns in many states across the nation.

Flat Lands and Flat Water

> The wagon jolted on, carrying me I knew not whither. . . .
> Between that earth and sky I felt erased, blotted out.
> — *Willa Cather, U.S. author,* My Ántonia, *1918*

Nebraska's lands were formed hundreds of thousands of years ago during the Ice Age. When the glaciers retreated, the land was transformed into a region of rolling prairies and plains with rich, fertile soil and an abundance of rivers and streams.

The state itself is about 430 miles (691 km) wide and 210 miles (338 km) long. It includes some of the region called the Great Plains that extends from Texas to Canada. Nebraska's land slopes gradually from its highest point in the southwest corner of the panhandle to its lowest point in the southeast corner of the state along the Missouri River.

The Regions

The rich soil in Nebraska's eastern lowlands and southern plains is well-suited to farming. This region is also naturally irrigated by the rivers and streams that empty into the Missouri River. The soil is so rich because it contains glacial till, the material glaciers left behind as they melted. The till was dissected, or cut, by the many streams that flowed over it. The majority of the state's population lives in the eastern part of the state.

Highest Point

Panorama Point
(unofficial name, in Johnson Township)

5,424 feet (1,653 m) above sea level

▼ *From left to right:* Nebraska marshland; a prairie dog; the distinctive Sand Hills; worn rocks in the Oglala National Grassland; a sod house in Gothenburg; Nebraska wheat.

The rest of Nebraska is in the Great Plains. This region contains the state's most distinctive topographical feature — the Sand Hills. They cover nearly 20,000 square miles (51,800 sq km), an area slightly smaller than West Virginia, and they are the largest expanse of sand dunes in North America. The rolling ridges and hills of sand absorb the rain and are held in place by natural grass cover. The region provides excellent grazing for cattle and yields wild hay used to feed livestock.

The High Plains are north and west of the Sand Hills. This lightly populated area includes rugged, forested land more characteristic of the neighboring states of Wyoming and Colorado. It also includes hundreds of small lakes. Pine Ridge is a spectacular cliff that marks the northern edge of the High Plains and extends into both South Dakota and Wyoming. As its name suggests, it is covered in evergreen trees, as is Wildcat Hills to the south. The High Plains area is home to many cattle ranches.

Rivers and Lakes

Due to the natural slope of the state, most Nebraska rivers run eastward and empty into the mighty Missouri River, which forms the state's eastern border and part of its northern border. In fact, the entire state is within the Missouri drainage basin.

The Platte River completely spans the state from west to east. The northern and southern branches originate in Wyoming and Colorado and converge near North Platte. Although it is the state's major river, the Platte is too shallow for navigation. With maximum widths nearing 1 mile (1.6 km), it has been described as "a mile wide and an inch deep."

The state's central area is drained by the Loup River and its system of streams that extend into the Sand Hills.

Average January temperature
Omaha: 22°F (-6°C)
Scottsbluff: 25°F (-4°C)

Average July temperature
Omaha: 78°F (26°C)
Scottsbluff: 74°F (23°C)

Average yearly rainfall
Omaha: 30 inches (76 cm)
Scottsbluff: 15 inches (38 cm)

Average yearly snowfall
Omaha: 32 inches (81 cm)
Scottsbluff: 38 inches (97 cm)

Major Rivers

Missouri River	2,315 miles (3,725 km)
Republican River	445 miles (716 km)
Niobrara River	430 miles (692 km)
Platte River	310 miles (499 km)
Loup River	290 miles (467 km)

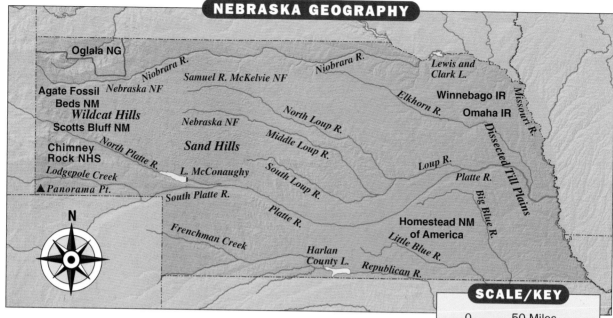

SCALE/KEY

0	50 Miles
0	50 Kilometers

NF National Forest

NG National Grassland

NHS National Historic Site

NM National Monument

IR Indian Reservation

▲ Highest Point

Mountains

The Loup empties into the Platte, as does the Elkhorn River, which drains much of the northeastern part of the state. The major river in the north is the Niobrara, which flows along the northern edge of the Sand Hills and empties into the Missouri. South of the Platte, the Republican, Little Blue, and Big Blue Rivers flow into Kansas.

Nebraska has more than two thousand lakes, but most are small. The largest are artificial reservoirs built along rivers to control flooding. The largest lake in the state is Lake McConaughy, which stretches 20 miles (32 km) in length and was formed when the Kingsley Dam was constructed on the North Platte River. Nebraska has 481 square miles (1,246 sq km) of water.

Climate

Due to its location in the center of the continent and its elevated but flat topography, Nebraska experiences weather extremes. Temperatures have reached 114° Fahrenheit (46° Celsius) in the summer and plunged as low as -25°F (-32°C) in winter. The state also has a history of alternating between floods and droughts, both of which have seriously affected local farmers.

Nebraska's blizzards pose the greatest threat to human and animal life, but tornadoes pose the greatest threat to property. Nebraska averages thirty-nine tornadoes each year.

DID YOU KNOW?

Nebraska has two national forests, the Nebraska National Forest, near Halsey and Chadron, and the Samuel R. McKelvie National Forest, near Valentine. Both forests have been created in part through the hand-planting of seedlings.

Plants and Animals

Forests currently cover just under 4 percent of the state's land. A natural scarcity of trees caused many early pioneers to build their houses from sod, or grassy earth, instead of wood. The trees that do grow naturally in the eastern part of the state include ash, oak, elm, willow, and cottonwood. In the west, pines and cedars predominate.

Of the natural prairie grasses that cover the Sand Hills, bluestem is the most common. Shorter grasses, including grama and buffalo grass, cover the dry lands in the western part of the state. Wildflowers, such as poppies, wild roses, violets, columbines, larkspurs, and sunflowers, add color to the landscape during the warm summer months.

Before the 1870s, the American bison was the dominant large mammal, but the great buffalo hunts of the 1870s nearly exterminated the species. The few that remain live mostly in wildlife refuges. Today one is more likely to see herds of antelope running freely, along with deer, coyotes, raccoons, badgers, opossums, rabbits, prairie dogs, foxes, and squirrels. Migrating birds, including sandhill cranes, frequent the Platte River.

Largest Lakes

Lake McConaughy
35,712 acres
(14,453 ha)

Lewis and Clark Lake
31,360 acres
(12,691 ha)

Harlan County Lake
13,248 acres
(5,361 ha)

▼ This view from Scotts Bluff shows how dry creek beds cut through short-grass prairie. In the distance are mesas, distinctive, flat-topped hills caused by erosion. Mesas are typical of the region.

The Heartland of Agriculture

> Without education, you're not going anywhere in this world.
>
> — *Malcolm X, civil rights advocate, in a 1964 speech*

Since the days of the pioneers, farming and ranching have been Nebraska's main sources of wealth. The land that was once home to millions of buffalo is now home to millions of cattle, and many of the native grasses have been replaced by vast fields of corn and wheat.

The importance of agriculture declined somewhat in the late twentieth century as service and manufacturing jobs became more prevalent. Nebraska's economy, however, still revolves around agriculture. Much of the state's commerce and industry involves processing and transporting farm and ranch products and providing services to those engaged in agriculture. Related industries, including the production of agricultural chemicals and the manufacturing of farming machinery, are further evidence of the importance of agriculture to Nebraska's economy.

Livestock

Nebraska remains one of the leading states in agricultural production. The state has more than fifty-four thousand farms — approximately 93 percent of the land is used for farming or ranching.

The state is also one of the world's major meatpacking centers. Some of the state's largest cattle ranches are located in the Sand Hills region of the central plains. The grasses found there, as well as locally grown corn products, play a vital role in fattening the cattle before they are sent to market. Hogs, poultry, and dairy products are produced mostly in the east. Sheep are raised in the east, as well as in the western panhandle area. Approximately two-thirds of Nebraska's farming income — almost $6 billion annually — comes from livestock and livestock products.

Top Employers (of workers age sixteen and over)	
Services	32.2%
Wholesale and retail trade	22.5%
Manufacturing	12.7%
Agriculture, forestry, and fisheries	8.3%
Transportation, communications, and utilities	8.1%
Finance, insurance, and real estate	6.7%
Construction	5.3%
Public Administration	3.9%
Mining	0.3%

▲ Nebraska cowboys
still herd Hereford
cattle on horseback,
using traditional
ranching practices.

Cash Crops

Crops account for approximately one-third of the state's farming income. Corn, the most valuable cash crop, is planted on more than 8,000,000 acres (3,237,600 ha) of land each year. Not surprisingly, the state's livestock are the largest consumers of the state's corn.

Nebraska farmers specialize in products naturally suited to the region. Soybeans and grain sorghum are grown in the eastern and southeastern regions, while the central plains are ideal for cultivating hay. Wheat farms can be found along the southern border and in the panhandle region. Other crops, including beans, oats, barley, potatoes, alfalfa, and sugar beets, are grown throughout the state.

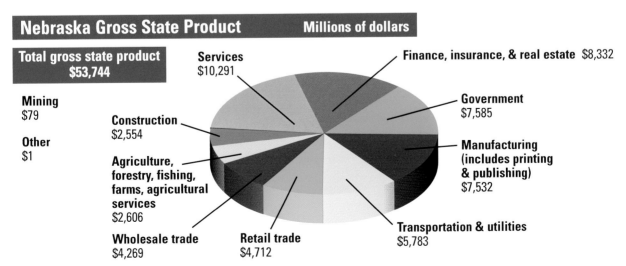

Nebraska Gross State Product   **Millions of dollars**

Total gross state product
$53,744

Services $10,291

Finance, insurance, & real estate $8,332

Mining $79

Other $1

Construction $2,554

Government $7,585

Manufacturing (includes printing & publishing) $7,532

Agriculture, forestry, fishing, farms, agricultural services $2,606

Transportation & utilities $5,783

Wholesale trade $4,269

Retail trade $4,712

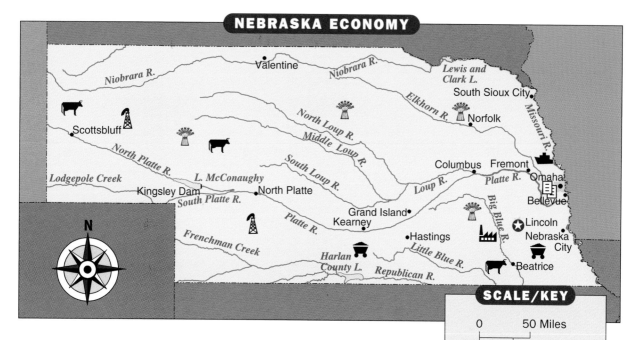

NEBRASKA ECONOMY

Dairy farming is also a significant enterprise. Most dairy farms are found in the northeastern region. While the number of dairy farms has decreased in recent years, the size of individual operations has increased.

Manufacturing

The main type of manufacturing in the state is food processing, particularly of meat and grain products. Among the most widely produced grain product exports are breakfast cereals, livestock feed, and baked goods.

Significant income is generated by manufacturing, including heavy machinery for farming or industrial use, as well as scientific and medical instruments. Printed and published materials, chemical and pharmaceutical products, and electrical equipment also contribute to the economy.

Transportation

Transportation by river, trail, rail, and road has played an essential part in the development of Nebraska. The Union Pacific tracks that lead west from Omaha were part of the nation's first transcontinental railway. Today, the Union Pacific is still in business and, along with the Burlington Northern Railroad, provides the majority of freight service in Nebraska.

Riverboats and barges transport the state's corn, grain, and animal products via the Missouri River.

Made in Nebraska

Leading farm products and crops
Livestock (cattle, hogs)
Corn
Grain sorghum
Wheat
Oats
Soybeans
Beans

Other products
Processed foods
Industrial machinery
Electrical equipment
Metal products

The state's largest shipping ports are Omaha, Nebraska City, and South Sioux City.

Major Airports

Airport	Location	Passengers per year (2000)
Eppley Airfield	Omaha	3,814,440
Lincoln Municipal	Lincoln	530,723

All together, Nebraska has about 93,000 miles (150,000 km) of roads and highways that stretch across the state. The main highway that runs east-west from Omaha to the Wyoming border is Interstate 80, which is a major thoroughfare for interstate trucking.

Employment

The greatest earnings in Nebraska are generated by the service sector, which includes health and business services and employs more Nebraskans than any other industry. Wholesale and retail workers make up the second-largest group of workers in the state.

One business of particular importance to Nebraska is insurance. More than thirty insurance companies have their headquarters in Nebraska. The largest of these companies is Mutual of Omaha, which is listed in *Fortune* magazine as one of the 500 largest and most profitable corporations in the United States. Union Pacific and ConAgra Foods are also among the "Fortune 500" firms based in Nebraska.

Natural Resources

Nebraska's primary resources include the fields of petroleum and natural gas that are found in the western and south-central regions. There are limestone quarries along the Missouri River, and sand and gravel are collected in the Platte and Republican River regions.

A Tall, Cool One

In 1927, Edwin E. Perkins of Hastings invented a powdered soft-drink mix, which he called Kool-Aid. He sold packages of the powder to local grocery stores. Demand grew quickly, and he was soon selling his product internationally. Kool-Aid made Perkins wealthy, and he donated a great deal of money to Hastings.

A Plain-Spoken State

> By their very nature, democracies recognize the right of people to lead their own lives, to resolve differences peacefully, and to live in a culture of their own choosing.
>
> — *U.S. Vice President Dick Cheney, 2001*

Nebraska voters approved their first constitution in 1866. After changing the constitution to allow non-white males the right to vote, Nebraska became a state in 1867. In 1875, voters replaced the constitution with one that limited the power of state government. Although many amendments have been passed since then, this constitution is still in effect today. A 1912 amendment gives people the "power of initiative," which means that citizens can propose constitutional amendments or changes in local statutes by petition.

Executive Branch

Nebraska voters elect the state's governor and five other executive branch officials. All are elected to four-year terms. The governor and lieutenant governor are limited to two consecutive terms, but they can serve an unlimited number of nonconsecutive terms. The governor appoints many members of state boards, commissions, and departments, but all members of the state board of education are elected by the voters. The governor has the power to veto any legislation passed by the legislature, but the veto can be overruled by a three-fifths vote of the legislature.

In 1986, the state made a first in U.S. history when both major parties nominated women to run for governor. Kay Orr defeated Helen Boosalis to become Nebraska's first woman governor and the first Republican woman governor in the United States.

Legislative Branch

Nebraska is the only state in the nation that has a unicameral legislature, meaning there is just one

DID YOU KNOW?

Nebraska's legislators are citizen legislators, which means that almost all of them have other jobs in addition to their work in the legislature. Each senator is paid $12,000 per year for serving in the legislature.

We the People

All persons are by nature free and independent, and have certain inherent and inalienable rights; among these are life, liberty and the pursuit of happiness. To secure these rights, and the protection of property, governments are instituted among people, deriving their just powers from the consent of the governed.

— *Nebraska Bill of Rights, 1875*

Elected Posts in the Executive Branch

Office	Length of Term	Term Limits
Governor	4 years	2 terms*
Lieutenant Governor	4 years	2 terms*
Secretary of State	4 years	None
Attorney General	4 years	None
State Treasurer	4 years	None
Auditor of Public Accounts	4 years	None

* These officials may serve no more than two consecutive terms within a twelve-year period. After a time-out of four years, they may run for office again.

lawmaking body, as opposed to the usual model with a senate and a separate house of representatives. Additionally, the legislature is nonpartisan. Candidates' political parties are not listed on the ballot, and leaders are not chosen based on their party membership. Voters elect one representative, called a state senator, from each of the state's forty-nine legislative districts.

The legislature meets every year. The regular sessions begin on the Wednesday after the first Monday in January. The sessions are limited to sixty days in even-numbered years and ninety days in odd-numbered years. The sessions may be extended by the senators themselves with a four-fifths vote. The governor may call a special session or the legislature may call one, if approved by a two-thirds vote.

Judicial System

The highest court in Nebraska is the supreme court, which is headed by a chief justice and includes six associate justices representing the state's six judicial districts. The court of appeals has six judges, while the state's twelve district courts have a total of fifty-five judges.

In 1964, a merit plan was introduced for judge selection to the supreme, appellate, and district courts of Nebraska. According to the plan, the governor selects a judge when a seat becomes

A Capitol Statue

The 19-foot (6 m) tall statue *The Sower*, which stands atop the state capitol in Lincoln, is visible from 20 miles (32 km) away due to the flatness of the prairies surrounding it. *The Sower* is a farmer scattering, or sowing, seeds.

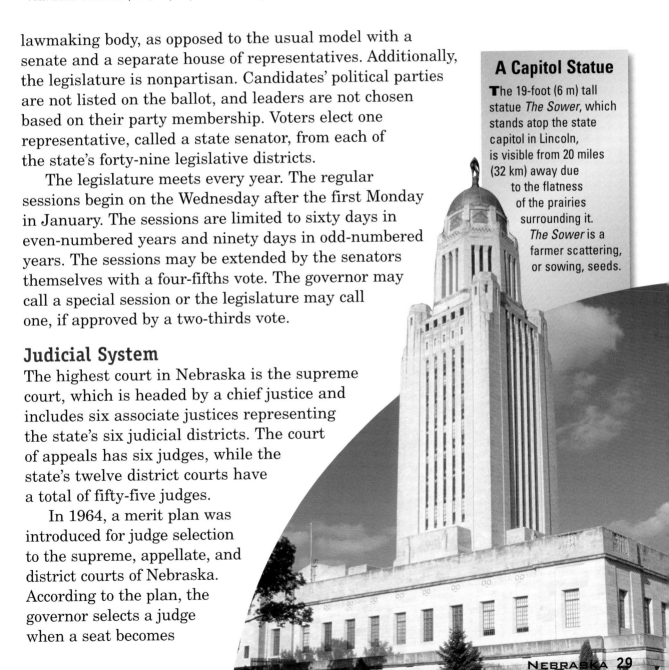

vacant. After three years on the bench, that judge must be approved by voters in a general election. If approved, the judge may then serve six more years. All judges must be approved by the voters every six years.

Nebraska has twelve districts in its county court system and fifty-nine county judges. The state's three largest counties (Douglas, Lancaster, and Sarpy) each have separate juvenile courts. The nine juvenile court judges are all subject to the merit plan.

Local Government
There are ninety-three counties in Nebraska, and sixty-six of them are governed by a board of commissioners made up of three to five members who are elected to four-year terms. The remaining twenty-seven counties are each governed by a board of supervisors. There are seven members on each board of supervisors, and those members are also elected to four-year terms.

Tribal/Sovereign Governments
Today the Omaha, Ponca, Santee Sioux, and Winnebago Indian nations all have independent tribal governments within Nebraska. These nations are governed by democratic tribal constitutions and tribal councils. In 1953, the U.S. Congress passed Public Law 280, which gave states the right to police and make laws in independent territories. Public Law 280 applied to Alaska, California, Minnesota, Nebraska, Oregon, and Wisconsin. Since that time, the Nebraska government has allowed the Omaha and Winnebago to run their own judicial and law enforcement agencies.

The State Capitol
The current capitol building in Lincoln was designed by Bertram G. Goodhue and is widely considered to be a great architectural achievement. Completed in 1932, the building consists of a cross within a square that forms four separate interior courtyards on the ground level. A 400-foot (122-m) domed tower rises from the center of the base and is topped

William Jennings Bryan
During the 1800s and early 1900s, the majority of Nebraska's representatives and senators were Republican. Among the notable exceptions were William Jennings Bryan (*above*), a Democrat who served in the U.S. House of Representatives from 1891 to 1895, and George W. Norris, a Republican in name only who served in the House and the Senate for a total of forty years from 1903 to 1943. Both men were liberal reformers who worked hard to help poor and disadvantaged Nebraskans.

State Legislature			
House	Number of Members	Length of Term	Term Limits
Unicameral	49 senators	4 years	2 consecutive terms

The White House via Nebraska

GERALD RUDOLPH FORD (1974–1977)

Born in Omaha on July 14, 1913, "Jerry" Ford became the 38th president of the United States on August 9, 1974. Ford's rise to the presidency was unusual because he was never actually elected to the office. While serving in the U.S. House of Representatives as a representative from Michigan, Ford was appointed vice president after Spiro T. Agnew resigned from office in 1973. The next year, President Richard M. Nixon faced impeachment because of the Watergate scandal. Nixon became the first president to resign from office, and Ford became president. From Nixon, Ford inherited a troubled economy, rising inflation, and energy shortages. Upon taking the oath of office, Ford said, "I assume the Presidency under extraordinary circumstances. . . . This is an hour of history that troubles our minds and hurts our hearts."

His presidency lasted just two and a half years — until January 1977. Ford was a popular and well-liked president, and although he did win the Republican nomination for the presidency in 1976, he lost the election to Jimmy Carter, a Democrat from Georgia. On the day of his inauguration, Carter began his speech by saying, "For myself and for our nation, I want to thank my predecessor for all he has done to heal our land."

by a 19-foot (6-m) bronze figure, *The Sower*, which represents the state's agricultural industry. Inside the building, visitors may see magnificent floor and ceiling mosaics by artist Hildreth Meiere. Her tile mosaics portray the fruits of Nebraska agriculture. Meiere considered these mosaics to be her greatest works.

Revenue

It wasn't until 1967 that Nebraska adopted a sales tax and an income tax. Today these taxes provide more than half of the state government's income. Other taxes include a gasoline tax, a corporate income tax, motor vehicle license fees, and insurance, liquor, and tobacco taxes. Nebraska also receives funding from federal grants and government programs.

A unique aspect of the state constitution is that it does not allow the government to acquire any debt greater than $100,000. Therefore, all payments for government spending must be made on a pay-as-you-go basis.

DID YOU KNOW?

In November 1992, 63 percent of Nebraska voters approved a constitutional amendment authorizing a state lottery. It became the nation's thirty-seventh lottery on September 11, 1993, when the first tickets were sold.

Cowboys and Cornhuskers

> In the sandhill country, where the going was tougher, leaner, and lonelier, and the folklore tougher, fatter, and more plentiful, history may be retraced in the amusements of the people.
>
> — *from* Nebraska: A Guide to the Cornhusker State, *1939*

Despite endless fields of grain and ranches where the cattle outnumber the state's people, Nebraska is more than just a farming state. From the original pioneers who built sod houses because there were no trees, to the progressive politicians who declared that the two-party system and the two-chamber legislature were ideas of the past, Nebraskans have always exhibited an independent streak and practical common sense.

The state's personalities range from rodeo cowboys to a U.S. president, and throughout the state, football fans are in no short supply. The state's great expanses have inspired prize-winning novelists, and several major movie stars have emerged from local playhouses. Nebraska's cities may not be big, but they do provide a busy, urban alternative to the calm silence of the open plains.

Growing Green

The Bessey Ranger District of the Nebraska National Forest, just outside the town of Halsey, contains the largest hand-planted forest in the nation. It covers 20,000 acres (8,094 ha) and is a popular site for hiking, camping, and picnicking.

▼ Jim Reinders and his family used thirty-eight cars to create Carhenge, near Alliance in western Nebraska.

Natural Attractions

Although Nebraska is not usually considered a major tourist destination, tourism contributes more than $2.7 billion to the state's economy each year. Many of the state's more popular attractions are natural wonders. Tourists flock to the state's eighty-seven parks and recreation areas, as well as to sites such as the

Agate Fossil Beds National Monument in Sioux County. Much of the state's natural splendor can be found in the northwestern region. Both of the state's partially hand-planted national forests attract visitors. The Toadstool Geologic Park, in the Oglala National Grassland, contains dramatic and surreal landscapes of eroded badlands and fossilized animal tracks that are 30 million years old. Badlands are areas where there are few plants and where erosion has created strange shapes in rock formations.

Some tourists come to see the sights along the old Oregon and Mormon Trails as well as other historical spots in the Platte River Valley, such as Chimney Rock National Historic Site or Scotts Bluff National Monument. Perhaps the most famous of these historical places is the home of one of Nebraska's most famous residents, Buffalo Bill Cody.

Museums and the Arts

The Joslyn Art Museum in Omaha is Nebraska's largest and most distinguished art museum. It has a large collection of ancient and modern works, as well as art from the frontier days and art objects created by Native Americans. Many of Nebraska's museums are dedicated to the state's pioneering history and the work of local artists. The Durham Western Heritage Museum, also in

▲ Scout's Rest Ranch, home of the famous Buffalo Bill Cody, is part of the Buffalo Bill Ranch State Historical Park near North Platte.

The Wheels of History

The National Museum of Roller Skating is the world's only museum dedicated exclusively to the history of roller skating and the roller skate. It is located in Lincoln.

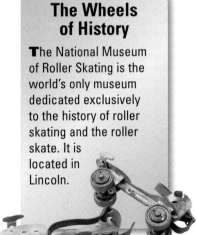

Omaha, the Museum of Nebraska History in Lincoln, and the Willa Cather State Historic Site in Red Cloud are all popular points of interest that highlight local history.

At the University of Nebraska in Lincoln, the Sheldon Memorial Art Gallery exhibits the work of nineteenth-century and contemporary artists. The collection includes photography and comic book illustrations. The University of Nebraska State Museum has a fossilized mammoth skeleton on display, just one of many in what is one of the nation's largest fossil collections. At the University of Nebraska campus in Kearney, the Museum of Nebraska Art features the work of artists from the state.

The cities of Omaha and Lincoln both have symphony orchestras, and since 1958 Omaha has had an opera company as well. Each year the Omaha symphony presents concerts for children, and in 2001, nearly forty thousand children attended performances by the symphony. National touring productions often visit the major cities, and local theater groups can be found throughout the state. The Lied Center for the Performing Arts, at the University of Nebraska in Lincoln, is one of Nebraska's most magnificent venues for live performance.

▼ The Joslyn Art Museum (*below*) is Nebraska's largest art museum and exhibits Native American, U.S., European, and ancient Greek and Roman art. The Durham Western Heritage Museum (*inset*) is housed in the old Union Station building in Omaha. One exhibit is a model train that is 100 feet (30 m) long.

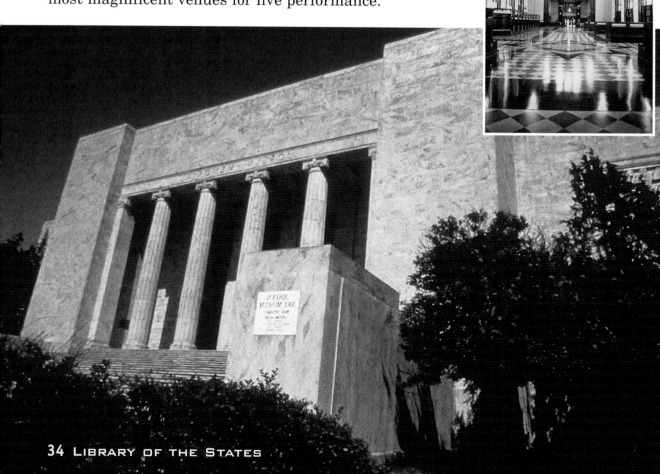

Omaha's Henry Doorly Zoo has the largest indoor rain forest, the Lied Jungle, as well as the largest indoor desert in the world. An IMAX theater and the Kingdom of the Seas Aquarium also make this a popular destination. In addition, the zoo maintains a conservation park and wildlife safari.

Literary Legacy

Nebraska's landscape has inspired a number of world-class writers. Three of these — Willa Cather, Bess Streeter Aldrich, and Mari Sandoz — wrote compelling tales that illuminated pioneer life from a woman's perspective. Sandoz particularly emphasized the strength and vitality of pioneer women. Cather's books, many of them modern classics such as *My Ántonia*, in which Cather uses the Nebraska plains during frontier times as a setting to explore such themes as human memory and the immigrant experience, have never gone out of print. Cather won the Pulitzer Prize in 1923 for her novel *One of Ours*. Loren Eisley, who spent his first 26 years in Lincoln, wrote evocatively about the prairie lands' unique history and culture in such books as *The Immense Journey*. Wright Morris, on the other hand, who grew up in the state, wrote about traveling everywhere, including Nebraska, often combining his writings with photography.

DID YOU KNOW?

The world's largest woolly mammoth fossil was unearthed in Lincoln County in 1922. Its skeleton, nicknamed Archie, is on exhibit in the Elephant Hall at the University of Nebraska State Museum in Lincoln.

Sports

Nebraska's wide-open spaces provide ample opportunity for outdoor recreation. Boating, swimming, and fishing are popular summertime activities on the state's numerous lakes, especially Lake McConaughy. On dry land, tourists and locals alike enjoy horseback riding, bicycling, camping, and hiking in the eighty-seven state parks and recreational areas.

No sporting activity in Nebraska, however, can compete with the state's love for football. The pride of the state is the University of Nebraska Cornhuskers football team. Since it won its very first game on November 27, 1890, the team has had the undying support of loyal fans. For the past forty years, it has been a major power in college football. In 2001, the team posted its fortieth consecutive winning season, the current National Collegiate Athletic Association record.

In addition to its famed football team, the University of Nebraska also has produced national championship teams in men's gymnastics and women's indoor track.

◀ Bikers enjoy Nebraska's many miles of level terrain.

Great Gatherings

The warm summer months are perfect for outdoor events, such as the many Native American gatherings that take place in the state each year. The Omaha Nation Powwow, held in Macy in late August, is one of the oldest powwows in the United States. Events include contests in which tribe members demonstrate traditional dances and ceremonial dress styles as well as drumming, singing, and war whoops. Powwows are a chance for Native American groups to celebrate their heritages and share them with members of other groups. Powwows also feature traditional arts and foods. In Niobrara, the Santee Sioux and Ponca tribes both host powwows, as do the Winnebago Indians in Winnebago.

A special event that happens in Nebraska each spring is the migration of the sandhill cranes. These birds travel hundreds of miles from their winter homes in Texas, New Mexico, California, and Mexico to a particular stretch of land along the Platte River in Nebraska. Nearly 70 percent of the world's population of these birds arrive in this one spot each spring. Nebraskans and bird-watchers from all over the world journey to the area between Grand Island and Sutherland to observe this spectacular gathering. The birds linger for a month and then move farther north to spend the summer in Alaska.

Noteworthy Nebraskans

> Destiny is not a matter of chance; it is a matter of choice.
> It is not a thing to be waited for; it is a thing to be achieved.
> — *William Jennings Bryan (1860–1925), lawyer*
> *and U.S. representative from Nebraska*

Following are only a few of the thousands of people who were born, died, or spent much of their lives in Nebraska and made extraordinary contributions to the state and the nation.

CHIEF STANDING BEAR
TRIBAL LEADER

BORN: *1829 or 1834, Nebraska Territory*
DIED: *circa 1908, Nebraska*

Ma-chu-nah-zah, as Standing Bear was known among his people, became a chief of the Ponca. The Ponca had been pushed south by the Dakota and, at the time of Standing Bear's birth, were living in a small strip of territory along the Niobrara River. The U.S. government mistakenly included this strip of land in territory it gave to the Dakota, who then raided the Ponca to evict them, killing one-fourth of the Ponca people. Federal Indian agents decided that the best way to settle the dispute was to remove the Ponca to Oklahoma. Although a delegation of ten Ponca chiefs who inspected the Oklahoma territory decided against the move, the U.S. government forced them to migrate anyway. In Oklahoma many Ponca died, including

Standing Bear's son. Following the traditions of his people, Standing Bear attempted to return his son's remains to their native territory. When federal officials tried to stop him in 1879, Standing Bear made an eloquent plea before U.S. district court judge Elmer Dundy. Dundy ruled that "an Indian is a person within the meaning of the law," and as such could not be detained without reason. Standing Bear and other Ponca returned to their homes in Nebraska, and the U.S. government redrew boundary lines, returning land to them.

BUFFALO BILL CODY
AMERICAN SHOWMAN

BORN: *February 26, 1846, Scott County, IA*
DIED: *January 10, 1917, Denver, CO*

William Frederick Cody was a rider with the Pony Express before becoming a scout and guide for the Union army

during the Civil War. Cody was involved in sixteen battles with Native Americans who resisted white settlement in the West. Cody's exploits were written up in a vivid style and captured the interest of the U.S. public. A natural showman, Cody gained notoriety for his adventures and took on the name Buffalo Bill. In 1878, Cody settled on a ranch near North Platte. His neighbors asked Cody to throw a party for the Fourth of July in 1882, and the show he put on, the Old Glory Blowout, has been described as the first rodeo. In 1883, he organized an exhibition that depicted life in the West. The "Wild West Show" premiered before an audience of eight thousand people in Omaha. The show was hugely successful and toured the United States and Europe for nearly twenty years.

WILLA CATHER
WRITER

BORN: *December 7, 1873, Winchester, VA*
DIED: *April 24, 1947, New York, NY*

Willa Sibert Cather's family moved to Nebraska when she was a child, finally settling in Red Cloud when she was ten. There, she grew up among immigrants from eastern and central Europe and Scandinavia.

After graduating from the University of Nebraska, Cather moved to Pittsburgh, where she taught high school and worked for a newspaper while writing poetry and fiction. Her first book of poetry was published in 1903, and her first book of short stories was published in 1905. By 1906, she was living in New York City and had become the managing editor for *McClure's Magazine*, a well-respected journal of the day. Cather left *McClure's* in 1912 to dedicate herself to writing. Her stories are filled with themes and characters remembered from her early years in Nebraska. In 1923, she won the Pulitzer Prize in fiction for her 1922 novel, *One of Ours*. Cather once said that to write, one must "find your own quiet center of life, and write from that to the world." Other famous works by Cather include *My Ántonia* (1918), *A Lost Lady* (1923), and *Death Comes for the Archbishop* (1927).

J.C. HALL
ENTREPRENEUR

BORN: *December 29, 1891, David City*
DIED: *October 29, 1982, Leawood, KS*

Joyce Clyde Hall, known as J.C., began working odd jobs when he was eight years old. By the time he graduated from high school, he was a small-time peddler of picture postcards. With the money he had saved up, he opened his own business in Kansas City in 1910. Two of his brothers joined him in the business, and they began printing their own cards. That business grew into the corporation now known as Hallmark Cards, the largest greeting-card company in the world. The company's slogan is "When You Care Enough to Send the Very Best." Since 1951 Hall's company has sponsored cultural and educational television productions with its *Hallmark Hall of Fame* series.

FRED ASTAIRE
DANCER AND ACTOR

BORN: *May 10, 1899, Omaha*
DIED: *June 22, 1987, Los Angeles, CA*

Born Frederick Austerlitz, Fred Astaire began his career as a child dancer in vaudeville with his sister Adele. Together, they went on to conquer Broadway before he became a movie star in the early 1930s. Astaire was paired with Ginger Rogers, and they thrilled the world with their dance routines. Astaire and Rogers starred in many popular films, including *Top Hat* (1935), *Swing Time* (1936), and *Shall We Dance* (1937). Astaire went on to star with Leslie Caron in *Daddy Long Legs* (1955) and with Audrey Hepburn in *Funny Face* (1957). In 1949, he won a special Academy Award for his achievement in film, but his talents were not always so obvious. It is said that after his first studio screen test, an executive evaluated his potential by writing, "Can't act, can't sing, a little bald, can dance a little."

MARLON BRANDO
ACTOR

BORN: *April 3, 1924, Omaha*

Marlon Brando's mother was a member of the community theater in his hometown, but he made his acting debut on Broadway in 1944. Three years later, he appeared to great acclaim in Tennessee Williams' play *A Streetcar Named Desire*. Having studied with the famous acting coach Stella Adler in New York City, he was one of the first stars to use "method acting." With his role as a biker in *The Wild Ones*, he became a symbol of rebellious youth. He won his first Oscar in 1954 for *On the Waterfront*, in which he said the famous line, "I coulda been a contender." He also starred in the 1951 film version of *A Streetcar Named Desire*, as well as in *Julius Caesar* (1953), *Guys and Dolls* (1955), and *The Godfather* (1972), for which he won, but did not accept, a second Oscar.

MALCOLM X
CIVIL RIGHTS ADVOCATE

BORN: *May 19, 1925, Omaha*
DIED: *February 21, 1965, New York, NY*

Born Malcolm Little, Malcolm X was the son of a Baptist minister. After his father's death and his mother's emotional breakdown six years later, Malcolm lived in a succession of foster homes and orphanages. By the age of twenty, he had been convicted of burglary in Boston and sentenced to seven years in prison. During those years in jail, he became interested in and studied the Nation of Islam and the teachings of its leader, Elijah Muhammad. Upon his release from prison in 1952, he rejected what he considered his slave name of Little and renamed himself Malcolm X. He joined a Black Muslim mosque in Detroit and quickly became a charismatic public speaker. He was later appointed a minister and national spokesman for the Nation of Islam. He spoke passionately of "Black Power," or African-American empowerment. Both his viewpoints and speeches were often controversial. In 1964, he ended his association with the Nation of Islam and made a life-changing pilgrimage to Mecca in Saudi Arabia. Through it all, crowds and controversy followed him until 1965, when he was assassinated while addressing a crowd in New York City.

JOHNNY CARSON
TV PERSONALITY

BORN: *October 23, 1925, Corning, IA*

John William Carson moved to Nebraska with his family when he was eight years old. He studied speech and radio at the University of Nebraska. After graduation, Carson

found work as a disc jockey at a radio station in Omaha and began appearing on local television. He eventually moved to Los Angeles, where he replaced Jack Paar as host of *The Tonight Show* in 1962. He soon became a fixture on late night television and successfully hosted the show for thirty years. He retired in 1992, and Jay Leno took over as host.

WARREN BUFFETT
FINANCIER

BORN: *August 30, 1930, Omaha*

Warren Edward Buffett is one of the world's wealthiest people. From an early age, Buffett showed signs of a talent for business and finance and made his first investment in stock at age eleven. He graduated from the University of Nebraska in 1950 and received a graduate degree from Columbia University in New York City a year later. After working in finance, first in Omaha and then in New York, he returned to Omaha and formed his own money management business, which was extremely successful. Eventually he bought a textile manufacturing company called Berkshire Hathaway, which went on to acquire insurance and other companies and is now worth billions of dollars. For most of his career, Buffett has lived in Omaha, in a house he bought more than forty years ago.

DICK CHENEY
U.S. VICE PRESIDENT

BORN: *January 30, 1941, Lincoln*

Richard B. Cheney began his public service under President Richard Nixon in 1969. He went on to serve as assistant to the president and White House chief of staff during the Gerald Ford administration, and then served six terms as the lone congressman from Wyoming. He also served as the secretary of defense from 1989 to 1993 and was awarded the Presidential Medal of Freedom by President George Bush in 1991. From 1995 to 2001, Cheney served as chief executive of a company that provided technology and services to oil and gas companies. In 2000, George W. Bush picked his father's former defense secretary to be his running mate on the Republican ticket. When Bush won the closely contested election, Cheney became vice president.

Nebraska
History At-A-Glance

1541
Francisco Vásquez de Coronado claims the Great Plains in the name of Spain.

1682
René-Robert Cavelier, Sieur de La Salle, claims the Louisiana Territory, including present-day Nebraska, for France.

1720
Pawnee kill Spanish explorers in Nebraska.

1739
Pierre and Paul Mallet arrive in present-day Nebraska and name the Platte River.

1803
United States acquires present-day Nebraska with Louisiana Purchase.

1804
Lewis and Clark pass through Nebraska as they explore the land acquired in the Louisiana Purchase.

1819
U.S. Army establishes Fort Atkinson in Nebraska.

1823
Bellevue trading post becomes first permanent non-Native settlement in Nebraska.

1834
Federal government designates Nebraska "Indian country."

1854
Federal government passes the Kansas-Nebraska Act, creating the Nebraska Territory and opening it to settlement.

1862
The Homestead Act spurs large numbers of U.S. settlers to move to Nebraska.

1865
Union Pacific Railroad begins building a transcontinental line in Omaha.

1600   **1700**   **1800**

1492
Christopher Columbus comes to New World.

1607
Capt. John Smith and three ships land on Virginia coast and start first English settlement in New World — Jamestown.

1754–63
French and Indian War.

1773
Boston Tea Party.

1776
Declaration of Independence adopted July 4.

1777
Articles of Confederation adopted by Continental Congress.

1787
U.S. Constitution written.

1812–14
War of 1812.

United States
History At-A-Glance

1867
Nebraska becomes 37th state.

1883
Nebraska women gain the right to vote in school board elections. Full suffrage rights granted by the state in 1917.

1917
Father Edward J. Flanagan opens Home for Homeless Boys, later Boys Town, in Omaha.

1918
Willa Cather's novel of Nebraska life, *My Ántonia*, is published.

1927
Nebraskan Edwin E. Perkins invents Kool-Aid.

1933
Nebraska governor Charles Bryan signs legislation suspending farm foreclosures until the end of the Great Depression.

1934
Nebraska adopts a unicameral legislature.

1939
Oil discovered in southeast region of state.

1974
Nebraska-born Gerald Ford becomes president when President Richard Nixon resigns.

1982
Initiative 300 passes, banning corporations from buying farms or ranches.

1987
Kay Orr becomes Nebraska's first woman governor.

2001
Nebraska-born Dick Cheney takes office as vice president.

1800   **1900**   **2000**

1848
Gold discovered in California draws eighty thousand prospectors in the 1849 Gold Rush.

1861–65
Civil War.

1869
Transcontinental railroad completed.

1917–18
U.S. involvement in World War I.

1929
Stock market crash ushers in Great Depression.

1941–45
U.S. involvement in World War II.

1950–53
U.S. fights in the Korean War.

1964–73
U.S. involvement in Vietnam War.

2000
George W. Bush wins the closest presidential election in history.

2001
A terrorist attack in which four hijacked airliners crash into New York City's World Trade Center, the Pentagon, and farmland in western Pennsylvania leaves thousands dead or injured.

▼ In 1914, buyers line up at the horse market in Omaha.

Festivals and Fun for All

Check web site for exact date and directions.

Autumn Festival: An Arts & Crafts Affair, Omaha

More than five hundred artists come together to exhibit and sell their creations at this annual autumn arts and crafts extravaganza.
www.visitomaha.com

Douglas County Fair & Expo, Omaha

A local tradition since 1858, the fair provides a family-friendly showcase for all sorts of talent — exhibitions, performances, and contests ranging from frog jumping to bull riding.
www.douglascountyfair.com

Grundlovs Fest, Dannebrog

The Nebraska town of Dannebrog was named after the Danish flag, and each June the locals celebrate their Danish heritage with this weekend festival. The celebration includes a parade with bands and floats, games, exhibits, pony rides, and, of course, Danish pastries.
www.dannebrog.org/html/festivals.html

Husker Harvest Days, Grand Island

The western corn belt's largest annual farm show and expo includes demonstrations, exhibits, arts and crafts, food, and entertainment. All combined, they make Harvest Days fun for the whole family.
www.huskerharvestdays.com

July Jamm, Lincoln

Downtown Lincoln hosts three days of music and fun at one of the Midwest's best blues festivals. This outdoor party features world-class musicians, fantastic foods, and artisans selling everything from paintings to pottery.
www.julyjamm.org

Lincoln Renaissance Fair, Lincoln

Step back in time to the Middle Ages and the days of kings, queens, castles, and knights. Performers in period costumes bring the past to life through exhibits, demonstrations, food, and games.
www.lincoln.org/cvb/entertain/renai.htm

Nebraska Czech Festival, Wilber

For more than forty years, the small town of Wilber has held a weekend celebration of Czech traditions. Live performances, food, games, exhibits, a beauty pageant, and a children's parade are all part of the fun.
www.ianr.unl.edu/ianr/saline/czech.htm

◀ Colorful folk costumes are a traditional part of Dannebrog's Grundlovs Fest.

▶ Strolling crowds enjoy the Omaha Summer Arts Festival.

Nebraska State Fair, Lincoln

The State Fair has been in business since 1859, even before Nebraska was a state. The State Fair takes place in late August and early September, and other events take place on the grounds year-round.
www.statefair.org

Nebraska State Square and Round Dance Convention, Hastings

This annual celebration of traditional dance includes live entertainment, crafts, clothing, exhibits, and lots of dancing.
www.sqdancer.com/nebraska/state

Nebraskaland Days, North Platte

The midsummer spectacular in North Platte is based on the Western-style extravaganza first mounted by Buffalo Bill Cody in 1882. The festival includes a rodeo, parades, live entertainment, barbeques, and dances.
www.nebraskalanddays.com

Omaha Summer Arts Festival, Omaha

Painters, woodworkers, sculptors, jewelry makers, and photographers display their goods for the public at vending booths. There are also exhibits for young artists, a children's fair, food booths, walking tours, and live entertainment.
www.summerarts.org/wsponsors.html

Oregon Trail Days, Gering

This three-day carnival offers a quilt show, live entertainment, a chili cook-off, square dancing, bed racing, parades, and a Western and wildlife art show.
www.oregontraildays.com

Swedish Festival, Stromsburg

Each year on the third weekend of June, the "Swede Capital of Nebraska" celebrates the summer solstice and all things Swedish. The festival includes traditional entertainment and Swedish foods.
www.stromsburgnebraska.com/festival.asp

West Nebraska Cowboy Arts Festival, Gering

The Gering Civic Center hosts this festival honoring the U.S. cowboy with musical performances, art exhibits, trade shows, and business expos. Awards are given for artistic works entered in several competitive categories.
www.westernartsfestival.com

Winnebago Tribal Powwow, Winnebago

Every year in late August, members of the Winnebago tribe gather to celebrate the 1866 homecoming of Little Priest, a famous Winnebago war chief. Members of the tribe compete in contests that showcase traditional dances, costumes, singing, and drumming.
www.winnebagotribe.com/PowWow.htm

Books

Ferris, Jeri. *Native American Doctor: The Story of Susan LaFlesche Picotte*. Minneapolis, MN: The Lerner Publishing Group, 1991. Susan LaFlesche Picotte grew up on the Omaha reservation in Nebraska and was the first Native American woman to earn a medical degree. This book tells the story of her life and work as a doctor and advocate for her people.

Myers, Walter Dean. *Malcolm X: A Fire Burning Brightly*. New York: Harper Collins Children's Books, 1999. Nebraskan Malcolm X was an important figure in American history, leading the "Black Power" movement of the 1960s. Walter Dean Myers, an award-winning author, tells the compelling story of Malcolm X's life and ideas in this biography.

Strait, Treva Adams. *Miss Adams, Country Teacher*. Lincoln, NE: J&L Lee & Company, 1993. When she was eighteen years old, Treva Adams began teaching school in a shack on the Nebraska prairie. Her memoirs paint a portrait of life on the prairie in the 1930s.

Welsch, Roger. *Omaha Tribal Myths and Trickster Tales*. Lincoln, NE: J&L Lee & Company, 1981. This collection of traditional Omaha stories will give readers insight into the way the Omaha people lived in the era before European settlement.

Willis, Charles. *A Historical Album of Nebraska*. Brookfield, CT: Millbrook Press, 1995. Learn more about the history and people of the Cornhusker State in this comprehensive history.

Web Sites

▶ Official state site
www.state.ne.us

▶ Official site of Lincoln Chamber of Commerce
www.lcoc.com

▶ Official site for the Nebraska Division of Travel & Tourism
www.visitnebraska.org

▶ Nebraska State Historical Society
www.nebraskahistory.org

▶ Nebraska Blue Book
www.unicam.state.ne.us/bluebook/index.htm

Note: Page numbers in *italics* refer to maps, illustrations, or photographs.